Introduction

ON THE CELTIC CHURCH

Nora K. Chadwick
Newnham College,
University of Cambridge

The Celtic Church is a subject which still has value for the development of modern thought. The proud continental folk of the period of the Celtic Church spoke of the British Isles as 'on the edge of the habitable globe'. St. Columba, the greatest saint of the Celtic Church, is believed to have died in Iona in 597, the very year in which St. Augustine arrived in Kent, to inaugurate a different order and discipline in our country, one which had its headquarters and its organisation in Rome.

Before a century had passed, the end of the Celtic Church was already in sight.

In 731, when the Venerable Bede wrote the closing words of his *Ecclesiastical History*, he rested happy in the reflection that all the countries of Britain and Ireland, with the exception of the Welsh, had forsaken their former separatism and accepted the Roman obedience.

The Celtic Church had passed like a dream in the night.

For Bede, the sun shone on a new day. Yet, despite his loyalty and devotion to the Roman Church, Bede was himself in a large measure a product of the Celtic Church. His gentleness, his unworldliness, his idealism, his love of stories of pure lives, sprang from his boyhood memories of the Northumbria created by St. Aidan and St. Cuthbert and the early church of Lindisfarne.

What then do we mean by the Celtic Church? Wherein does it differ from the Church which claims to have superseded it?

Nearly a millennium-and-a-half has passed since it flourished, and it may well seem a far-off and fleeting memory, too remote from our troubled world to have a message for us today. Shall I confess the truth? It is because of its lasting beauty.

Bede tells us that when King Edwin was debating with his nobles of Northumbria in 627 as to whether they should accept Christianity, an unnamed member of the King's Council made a memorable speech. It is deservedly Bede's best-known piece of writing, but I beg you to forgive me for once again quoting it here, because it expresses my hope that the Age of the Saints in the Celtic Church is a subject which merits another book.

The Celtic Church of the Age of the Saints, as we see it in their gentle way of life, their austere settlements and their island retreats, the personalities of their saints, and the traditions of their poetry, expresses the Christian ideal with a sanctity and a sweetness which has never been surpassed.

The present life of man, O king, seems to me, in comparison with that time which is unknown to us, like the swift flight of a sparrow through the room in which you sit at supper in winter round the fire, while the wind is howling and the snow is drifting without. It passes swiftly in at one door and out through another, feeling for the moment the warmth and shelter of your palace; but it flies from winter to winter and swiftly escapes from our sight. Even such is our life here, and if anyone can tell us certainly what lies beyond it, we shall do wisely to follow his teaching.

Reproduced by the kind permission of Oxford University Press, publishers of Dr. Chadwick's *The Age of the Saints in the Early Celtic Church* (1961).

Chapter 1

FRONTRUNNERS

Who was the first Christian missionary to the British Isles? No one knows.

There are, of course, plenty of legends. There are stories about Joseph of Arimathea and others of the first generation of Christians landing in various places.

Some believe Christianity was introduced by Roman legionaries. *A Life of Germanus*, written in AD 480, tells the story of legionary Alban, who became *Saint* Alban. Having been baptised as a Christian, Alban was executed in the third century for sheltering a Christian priest. But Alban must have been exceptional; both history and archaeology are against the Roman legions as a source of Christianity. The Roman army of occupation "seems to have been wholly uninfluenced by Christianity during the first three centuries AD". Mithraism was the religion of the legions.[1]

There is, however, no shortage of evidence that there were small Christian settlements in both Ireland and Britain relatively early in the Roman period. Traces of Christian churches built as early as AD 360 have been discovered. Those who led the reaction against Christianity in the imperial reign of Julian the Apostate found themselves up against a sizeable minority.[2] As early as AD 200, Tertullian of Carthage in *Against the Jews* boasted that "parts of Britain inaccessible to the legions" had been "conquered for Christ".

So who *were* the earliest missionaries, if they were not legionaries? Merchants, traders, ordinary people.

It is probable that most of the merchants came from Gaul (France). A large wooden church in Glastonbury survived for centuries and may well have been built before the end of the first century.[3]

Under Roman rule a man could travel from Berwick [the northernmost town in England] to Babylon [located in present-day Iraq] without crossing a single international frontier. There was an infrastructure of roads that would have been as useful to traders as they were for soldiers. Traders came to Britain from other parts of the Empire, and left Britain for regions of the Empire where the religion of Jesus Christ had taken hold.

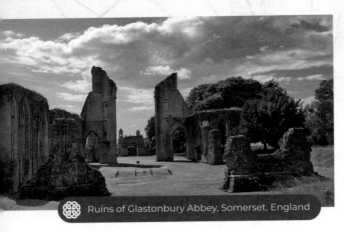
Ruins of Glastonbury Abbey, Somerset, England

The Gospel of the Nazarene made compelling listening around the hearths of traders in many parts of Britain.

If this was true of Britain, was it true of Ireland, outside of the Roman Empire?

The Roman historian Tacitus was the son-in-law of Agricola, Governor of Britain AD 77-84. In his *Life of Agricola* Tacitus paints a glowing picture of both the economy and civilisation of Ireland, comparing it favourably with Britain. He details the trade routes that linked Ireland with parts of the Empire, apart from Britain. Merchants brought Christianity to Ireland, as, perhaps, did Irish raiders returning from incursions into Wales and Scotland.

In the persecutions by the Roman authorities in the third century, many British Christians both suffered and died. According to *The Acts of the Council of Arles* five Britons attended the Council at Arles in AD 314. Third-century Roman writers Origen and Hippolytus both mention that Christianity had penetrated the British Isles. When Constantine called the Council of Nicaea in AD 325 to define Christian belief, the British were among those listed by Athanasius as accepting its decrees. The prominent Christian heretic, Pelagius, was born in Britain (c. AD 380), though his reputation as a theologian and a heretic was made in far-away Rome. Nevertheless, the spread of the Pelagian heresy in the British Isles caused concern in church circles on the Continent. As a result of this concern, in AD 431 Ireland was visited by Palladius, a bishop from Auxerre in France.[4] Palladius landed at Vatry in County Wicklow. He encountered Christian communities in eastern Ireland from Wicklow northwards to South Antrim.

> Merchants brought Christianity to Ireland, as, perhaps, did Irish raiders returning from incursions into Wales and Scotland.

Within a year Palladius was dead.

Soon another missionary had set sail from Gaul, bound for Ireland.

Palladius had been concerned with heresy in the small number of Christian communities that already existed.

The new missionary was on fire with an ideal.

The ideal?

To win the mass of the Irish people for the cause of Christ. His enemy was heathenism rather than heresy.

He stood in the apostolic tradition stretching back through to the very earliest champions of the cause of Christ.

His name was Patrick.

REFERENCES:

1. F. F. Bruce, *The Spreading Flame: The Rise and Progress of Christianity From its First Beginnings to the Conversion of the English* (1958), p. 353.

2. D. L. Edwards, *Christian England* (Revised Edition, 1989), pp. 18, 19; E. G. Bowen, *The Settlements of the Celtic Saints in Wales* (University of Wales, 1954), pp. 14-15.

3. Edwards, op. cit., p. 20.

4. Jakob Streit, *Sun and Cross: From Megalithic Culture to Early Christianity in Ireland* (1993), p. 67.

St. Patrick's Breastplate

Christ be with me, Christ within me,
Christ behind me, Christ before me,
Christ beside me, Christ to win me,
Christ to comfort and restore me.

Christ beneath me, Christ above me,
Christ in quiet, Christ in danger,
Christ in the hearts of all that love me,
Christ in the mouths of friends and strangers.

Chapter 2

PATRICK AND CELTIC CHRISTIANITY

The story of the Christian evangelisation of the British Isles really begins with Patrick.

The Christianity that existed before his arrival in AD 432 was weak and esoteric: weak enough in Britain, for example, to have been ignored by the Anglo-Saxon invaders who rushed into the power vacuum created by the departure of the Roman legions. The heathen invaders found no problem in making a complete break with the Roman past. They even renamed the days of the week after their own gods.

That the invaders did not succeed in re-imposing heathen religion and culture was because, in the century in which the legions departed, a vibrant, missionary-minded Christian movement had taken hold of Ireland. It was rendered the more compelling because, in doctrine and practice, it was far closer to New Testament Christianity than the mix of paganism and bowdlerised Christianity launched by the Roman Emperor Constantine. Previously a worshipper of the "Unconquered Sun", Constantine began to impose his new mishmash religion on the Empire after AD 313.[1]

By contrast, the Christianity of the Celtic missionaries Patrick, David, Columba and Aidan was a great light in a dark age. The Celtic Church of these men and their successors was responsible for evangelising first

Ireland, then Britain. From beacon-light religious settlements like Iona (Scotland) and Bangor (Ulster), missionaries were sent into continental Europe to places as far distant as Switzerland, Milan (Italy), Galicia (northern Spain) and Kiev (Ukraine).[2]

Decades before Patrick, Eusebius, the father of church history, in his *Life of Constantine*, commented on the cynical motives that prompted "conversion" to the Emperor's religion. There were few such hidden inducements to cause the Irish and the Britons to convert to the creed of the Celts. Two centuries after Eusebius another church historian, Bede of Jarrow (circa 673-735), "was conscious of the debt the English owed to saints such as Columba and Aidan, and loved to contrast their holiness with the 'slothfulness' of the Christians of his own day".[3] And this went against the grain for Bede. He was a legatee of Constantine, not the Celts. He was a spiritual descendant of Augustine, not Patrick.

The purer, Bible-based faith of Columba and Aidan to which Bede gave credit was introduced by Patrick. But, against the claims made for him by apologists writing centuries later, Patrick was emphatic that there were Christians in Ireland before his arrival. He wrote this in a letter: "In the days of old the law of God was well planted and propagated in Ireland; I do not wish to take credit for the work of my predecessors; I share the task with all those whom God has called . . . to preach the Gospel."[4]

The letter of which this was part was written by Patrick to Coroticus, King of Strathclyde. The letter rebuked him for a raid on Ireland which had resulted in the death of some of Patrick's converts and in the enslavement of others to the Picts. The letter to King Coroticus is one of only two primary historical sources generally accepted as having come from the hand of Patrick. The other is Patrick's autobiography, *Confessions*.

> The purer, Bible-based faith of Columba and Aidan to which Bede gave credit was introduced by Patrick.

So, who was Patrick?

Patrick was the son of a Roman British deacon, Calpurnius, and the grandson of a priest, Potitus. As a free-born provincial, Patrick was a Roman citizen.

In his *Confessions* Patrick identifies his birthplace as his father's estate at *Bannavem Taberniae*. There has been much speculation as to where this could have been. All we can tell from the context is that it was on or near the west coast of Britain – somewhere between the Bristol Channel and the Solway Firth!

In AD 405, when Patrick was 16, the Irish King Niall ventured on a warlike expedition to Britain. Among those captured and enslaved was Patrick. In Ireland he was bought by Milinc, a landowner at Slemish, near Ballymena in County Antrim.

For six years Patrick tended the herds of Milinc. Then he escaped. Taking advantage of a well-known trade route, he sailed to Gaul. While he was a slave Patrick discovered God in a fresh, new way. In Gaul this experience was further enlivened by a change in his life; a genuine Christian conversion. This gave him a hunger for biblical knowledge and theological training.

Lerins Abbey, France

In *Confessions* Patrick mentions the island of Lerins. Located in the Mediterranean off southern Gaul, Lerins was a centre "where monks from the Near East thronged".[5] It was viewed by Rome with great suspicion. The Coptic Christianity of Egypt was the dominant influence there. Coptic Christianity was derived directly from Jerusalem, not Rome. Its beliefs and practices were distinctly dissimilar from those of Constantine's Church. Hence it is likely that Celtic Christianity owes something to the Copts. But if the foundation of Celtic Christianity was Coptic, the evidence suggests that Patrick and Columba built an imposing and distinctive edifice upon it.[6] "The special form of sanctity

Auxerre Clock Tower, France

practised by the saints of the Celtic Church . . . could never have become a widespread movement without the communion and stimulus which they derived from the early Church through the written Word."[7]

Patrick's period at Lerins and his passion for Scripture almost certainly account for his independence of Rome.

After a period of years Patrick returned to his homeland. No sooner had he arrived than he received a vision that he was needed to preach the Gospel of Christ in Ireland, the land of his former captivity.

Patrick did not immediately heed the Macedonian-type cry, "Come over to Ireland and help us." Though he described himself as "the bond-servant of God", Patrick's autobiography is full of indications that he had an acute sense of personal inadequacy. It was this sense that led him, prior to his expedition to Ireland, to seek a formal training for the task ahead of him. For this he went to Auxerre (Gaul, France), a Christian centre – most unlike those around it – noted for its piety.

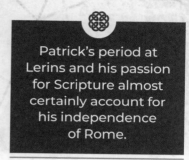

Patrick's period at Lerins and his passion for Scripture almost certainly account for his independence of Rome.

After a period of training Patrick was ordained as a deacon by Amator, Bishop of Auxerre. Following his ordination, he shared his vision to carry the Gospel to the Irish with the bishop. It would appear that the bishop gave him no encouragement. Patrick's Latin was poor, he lacked polish, and he, as he himself admitted, was "unsuitable for the task".

When a bishop was chosen to go to Ireland in AD 431 it was Palladius, not Patrick. The untimely death of Palladius enabled Patrick to follow his vision.

Over 40 now, Patrick was about to embark upon his life's work.

REFERENCES:

1. See F. F. Bruce, *The Spreading Flame: The Rise and Progress of Christianity From its First Beginnings to the Conversion of the English* (1958), p. 293 et seq.

2. D. L. Edwards, *Christian England* (revised edition, 1989), p. 54; *The Oxford History of Christianity* (ed.) John McManners (1993), p. 98; Jakob Streit, *Sun and Cross: From Megalithic Culture to Early Christianity in Ireland* (1993), pp. 179-191; Nora K. Chadwick, *The Age of the Saints in the Early Celtic Church* (Oxford University Press, 1961), pp. 58-59.

3. R. A. Markus, "From Rome to the Barbarian Kingdoms (330-700)", *The Oxford History of Christianity* (ed.) John McManners (1993), pp. 71, 98.

4. Jakob Streit, op. cit., p. 68.

5. Ibid., pp. 168-9; A. Lang, *A History of Scotland* (second edition, 1900), vol. 1, pp. 26-27; N. K. Chadwick, *The Age of the Saints* (Oxford, 1961), pp. 10-11; Hugh Williams, *Christianity in Early Britain* (Oxford, 1912), pp. 245-251.

6. Ibid., pp. 66-67, 70, 168-171.

7. N. K. Chadwick, op. cit., p. 37.

Chapter 3

PATRICK IN IRELAND

Whatever the Celtic Church stood for, it made the Roman Church angry.

A century after Patrick, Rome would launch an attack on the Celtic communities in Gaul. The reason given was the threat posed by the "peculiar Irish customs" – liturgies, observances and rites of baptism – that were totally at variance with those sanctioned by the increasingly powerful Bishop of Rome.[1]

These differences of belief and custom were preached and practised by Patrick. His long periods of study, first at Lerins, then at Auxerre, had given rise to them. Rooted in the New Testament, these distinctives derived from Jerusalem, not Rome. The Celts owed more to the Copts than to Constantine.

In his ministry in Ireland – from AD 432 to his death c. AD 460 – Patrick's task was to lighten the darkness of heathenism. His enemies were the Druids. And, preparatory to evangelising the masses, his first task was to tackle the kings. To assist him Patrick appointed sub-bishops: missionaries noted for their piety and sense of commitment rather than church governors.

The Druids were the custodians of the pagan lore of Ireland as of other Celtic lands. With their direct line to occult forces they represented a major threat. Many of the Celtic prayers extant invoke the power of the Trinity against the powers of Satanic darkness. Behind their pantheon of gods, the Druids, in fact, worshipped "the creative forces in nature, universe and man". The sun was the embodiment of their highest divinity. With their mix of occult dabbling, and their emphasis on the oneness of man, nature and "Earth Mother", they appear to us as distinctly "New Age". When Patrick landed to begin preaching Christ to the Irish, "Druidism was at the height of its power and development."[2]

The Ireland of AD 432 was divided into a number of tribal regions, each of which was ruled by a king. Beyond the tribal kings were more powerful provincial kings ruling the major regions of Munster, Connaught, Leinster, Meath and Ulster. Beyond the regional kings, between AD 379 and AD 405 the high kingship came into existence. In AD 432 the High King was Laoghaire (pronounced *Leary*), the son of Niall. He had acceded in AD 428 and was to reign in Tara for thirty-six years.

Aerial view of the Hill of Tara, an archaeological complex, County Meath, Ireland

It is likely that the High King at Tara was the first target of Patrick's evangelism. He must certainly have posed a challenge. The Druids, who saw the arrival of Patrick and his friends as the beginning of their end, advised the destruction of this new Christian champion. King Laoghaire would appear to have struck a compromise. He settled on a policy of toleration towards Patrick and his Christian clerics, but stopped short of actual conversion to Christianity.

It is likely that, from Tara, Patrick and his company of Gaulish and British assistants made contact with the Christian communities on the east coast of Ireland visited by Palladius during the previous year.

Tradition has it that, from some cove north of the site of Drogheda, Patrick sailed to Ulster, putting ashore near the mouth of Strangford Lough. From here Patrick's party made for the fortress of the local chieftain, Dichu, located where Downpatrick now stands. The chieftain's wife was the daughter of Patrick's former master, Milinc. Both the chieftain and his wife embraced the Gospel and were baptised.

Nearby, Patrick established his first church and Christian community at what is now Saul.

From Saul Patrick made for Slemish with a view to winning Milinc himself to the cause of Christ. There is a curious story that, on hearing of his former slave's approach, Milinc, a deeply superstitious man, set fire to his wooden house and died in the inferno.

From his base in Saul, Patrick evangelised an area that included what is now County Down and South Antrim. Here his evangelism met with outstanding success. It has been conjectured that the ground had been prepared for Patrick by Ninian's missionaries who had crossed from Whithorn in Galloway (Scotland).

Patrick and his missionaries invariably preached to the king-chieftain before preaching to his subjects. Despite lack of success with the High King at Tara, Patrick found some members of his family more responsive. Among the kings converted was Conall, brother of Laoghaire. After Conall's conversion, Meath embraced Christianity. With conversions came church building.

Next Patrick trekked west to Connaught. On his way he destroyed the stone idol of Crom Cruaich on the Plain of Slecht. At Croghan, the seat of the King of Connaught, Patrick baptised two daughters of the High King. A catechism is extant that is believed by many to have been put by Patrick to the two women:

Do you believe that by baptism you cast away the sin
of your father and mother?
Do you believe in repentance after sin?
Do you believe in life after death?
Do you believe in the resurrection and the day of judgement?
Do you believe in the unity of the Church?

It took Patrick seven years to evangelise Connaught. One year he spent the forty days of Lent on the Hill of the Eagle, now called Croagh Patrick, which rises 2,510 feet out of Clew Bay.

By AD 443 Patrick was back in Ulster. In that year it is believed that he founded the church and monastic settlement at Armagh, which was to become the ecclesiastical centre for Ireland and, during one period, for the whole of the British Isles.

Ulster, Meath and Connaught were the main centres of Patrick's evangelism. Nevertheless, "there is adequate evidence in ancient records that he visited Munster and Leinster as well."[3] Hence, by the time he resigned his episcopate at Armagh in AD 457, it is likely that Patrick presided over an Ireland that can be considered predominantly Christian.

Tradition has it that he retired to Saul, his first centre in Ulster, established some twenty-five years previously; that he died there on 17 March 461; and that he was buried in the vicinity of what is now Downpatrick Cathedral.

Today – within sight of Saul, his landing place on Strangford Lough and Downpatrick – a vast monolith to Patrick has been erected atop an imposing hill.

Few figures in history have so impressed their personalities upon a nation as did Patrick on Ireland. But Patrick was a self-effacing man. He concludes his *Confessions* with these words:

"I pray those who believe and fear God, whosoever has deigned to scan or accept this document, composed in Ireland by Patrick the sinner, an unlearned man to be sure, that none should ever say that it was my ignorance that accomplished

Cathedral in Downpatrick, Northern Ireland

any small thing which I did or showed in accordance with God's will; but judge ye, and let it be most truly believed, that it was the gift of God. And this is my confession before I die."

REFERENCES:

1. Jakob Streit, *Sun and Cross: From Megalithic Culture to Early Christianity in Ireland* (1993), pp. 179-191.
2. Ibid., pp. 58-64, 65.
3. F. F. Bruce, *The Spreading Flame: The Rise and Progress of Christianity From Its First Beginnings to the Conversion of the English* (1958), p. 382.

Chapter 4

COLUMBA IN SCOTLAND

While the disciples of Ninian of Whithorn may have had a hand in preparing part of Ulster for Patrick's evangelism, Patrick bemoaned the fact that the Southern Picts on the Scottish side of the North Channel – introduced to Christianity by Ninian – had reverted to paganism.

Ninian of Whithorn, a saint before Patrick, is a man of mystery today. Whithorn, where Ninian built his great monastery, is on the Wigtown Peninsula, not far from Stranraer. Part of the mystery about Ninian is whether he was "Roman" or "Celtic".

Ninian was born in the second half of the fourth century and had died before Patrick began to evangelise Ireland. He had a vast impact in his own lifetime. That much is generally accepted. The rest is confusion. And the confusion arises from the fact that the three historical sources from which we derive our information about Ninian were written centuries after his death, and therefore cannot be considered "primary". The first is Bede's *A History of the English Church and People* (written more than two centuries after Ninian's death). The second is a long eighth-century Latin poem compiled by a monk called Alcuin (AD 735-804). The third is a biography of Ninian written by Reginald of Durham, who visited Whithorn in 1164.

Ninian's college, called *Candida Casa*, was dedicated to Martin of Tours. In the days of Celtic Christianity new monastic sites either bore the name of their founder or of the founder of the parent monastery. Hence it can be assumed that Ninian received his education at Tours. This would place him in the same tradition as Patrick. However, Bede believed that Ninian was trained in Rome; and that would place him in the other tradition. To one modern authority Ninian, like Columba, was unquestionably in the Celtic tradition and Whithorn, like Iona, a "strategic centre" for the distinctive Celtic culture and theology.[1]

Ninian was the son of a baptised tribal chief in the district around the Solway Firth. In the period following the withdrawal of Roman troops from Hadrian's Wall, he took advantage of the stable government ensured by the Romano-British families who dominated Carlisle to evangelise the area. Either Ninian or his students may have established settlements further north in the Strathclyde region, and even in Ulster.

Sadly, whatever Ninian's beliefs may have been, his influence would appear to have died with him. Columba "had to convert Scotland and Northumberland afresh from Iona in the sixth century".

No one has ever questioned Columba's Celtic credentials. He had received his theology by way of Patrick, the Lerins community and the Eastern Mediterranean.[2]

He was the prime mover in bringing the various peoples of Scotland to the cause of Christ. Down to the eighth century Columba and his successors were the acknowledged leaders of the Irish (Celtic) Church.[3] It was as a direct result of Columba's impact that Rome began to feel threatened by the independent Church, declaring it to be "in error".[4]

There are four main sources on the life of Columba. The first two are biographies written by his successors as Abbot of Iona: Cummine (AD 657-669), who had known Columba personally; and Adomnan, Abbot from AD 679, who wrote within eighty years

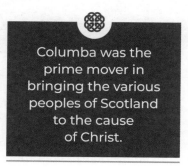

Columba was the prime mover in bringing the various peoples of Scotland to the cause of Christ.

of Columba's death. Added to these are the accounts of Columba in Bede's *Ecclesiastical History* and the anonymous *Columba: An Old Irish Life*, written in the tenth century. The latter appears in translation in the appendix to volume 2 of Professor W. F. Skene's three-volume *Celtic Scotland*, published 1886-90.

The best available primary source in print, however, is *Adomnan's Life of Columba*, edited by A. O. Anderson and M. O. Anderson and published by Thomas Nelson in 1961. Nora Chadwick considers that we are particularly fortunate to have Adomnan's *Life*; not only was Adomnan a successor of Columba on Iona but he shared the royal ancestry of the saint and, hence, had access to family memories and archives.[5]

Ian Finlay, Columba's most recent biographer, comments on the "atmosphere of miracle" in the biographies of Columba written by the abbots who succeeded him. This has to be penetrated in order to recognise the outline of fact.

Columba was born near Lough Garton, Donegal, on 7 December 521. On his mother's side he was descended from kings of Leinster. On his father's side he was descended from Niall and the high kings of Tara.

Historic Iona Abbey

Columba received the equivalent, for his time, of the best university education. At 24 he completed his studies under Finian of Clonard and Finian of Moville. Having founded a religious settlement at Derry, Columba, turned 40, set off with twelve companions to evangelise the Picts in AD 563. The direct distance by sea from Derry to Iona was about 100 miles. Early sources suggest that Columba and his friends crossed the Irish Channel in coracles of wicker and hide. Modern biographers suggest that he must have used a wooden craft. Whatever his means of conveyance, on the voyage north, Columba landed briefly in Argyle, decided against settling on the islands of Jura and Colonsay, and made for Iona, separated by a narrow channel from Mull. Conall, King of Dalriada, made a grant of Iona to Columba.[6]

Columba and his companions landed in a creek now known as Port of the Coracle and built a Celtic monastery, the site of which is commemorated by one of the famous High Crosses. Soon the original company was joined by scores, perhaps hundreds, of missionaries from Ireland. Iona – soon to become the headquarters of the Celtic Church – was humming with activity. But Iona's monasteries and abbeys, from the first so different and apart from those of Rome, were intended as a centre of operations, not a retreat. From there Columba, in Bede's words, "converted the nation to the faith of Christ by preaching and example".

Columba began his evangelism by targeting the Picts. Despite the hysteria of the Druids, King Bruide, whose fort-city was near the site of Inverness, became a Christian. After nine years among the Picts, Columba returned to the Britons and the Scots. Aidan was actually ordained as a king-priest on Iona. In company with Aidan, Columba returned to Ireland for a time, establishing a federation of Christian settlements. Somehow the great saint also found time for copying out the Scriptures, and for writing poetry.[7]

Later, another Aidan (died AD 651) was the Iona missionary who established Lindisfarne, the holy isle from which the kingdom of Northumbria was won for Christ. Aidan's successors sent missionaries south into England and north into the coastlands of eastern Scotland, establishing Columban settlements in Edinburgh and as far north as St. Andrews. Finan (who died in AD 661) was an Iona-trained missionary

The Holy Island, Lindisfarne

who, from Lindisfarne, carried Christianity beyond the frontiers of Northumbria into the lands conquered by the Saxons. In the process two Saxon chieftains were baptised.

Abbots Cummine and Adomnan both report Columba's prophecy that Iona would be venerated by kings of many nations – and by "other churches". Ian Finlay speculates, Did he mean Rome?[8]

Columba died on 9 June 597, aged 76. Adomnan, who wrote his *Life of Columba* in AD 688, noted that his death took place on a Saturday and that his final words to his servant were: "This day is called in the sacred books 'Sabbath', which is interpreted 'rest'. And truly this day is for me a Sabbath, because it is my last day of this present laborious life. In it, after my toilsome labours, I keep Sabbath."[9] Columba had always venerated the "divine commandments", and did so even with his final words.[10]

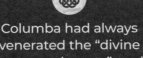

Columba had always venerated the "divine commandments", and did so even with his final words.

Summarising Columba's life, Ian Finlay remarks that the success of his evangelism was proof enough of the quality of the man. But Finlay is left with a question . . .

By raising the profile of the Celtic Church, Columba had directly challenged the authority of Rome. In the very year of Columba's death Pope Gregory sent Augustine as much to subdue Celtic "independence" as to convert the heathen Saxons. "In his lifetime Columba had success in plenty, but it might be held that the cause of the Church he founded in the long run was lost, and that the doom of it lurked in the heart of his success. . . ."[11]

REFERENCES:

1. N. K. Chadwick, *St. Columba* (Iona, 1963), pp. 14-15.
2. N. K. Chadwick, op. cit., pp. 8-9; Jakob Streit, *Sun and Cross: From Megalithic Culture to Early Christianity in Ireland* (1993), p. 174; N. K. Chadwick, *Studies in the Early British Church* (1958), pp. 4-5. See also F. F. Bruce, *The Spreading Flame* (1958), pp. 365-9, and E. G. Bowen, *The Settlements of the Celtic Saints in Wales* (University of Wales, 1954), pp. 19, 21-23.
3. Streit, op. cit., pp. 174-6.
4. Michael Sheane, *The Twilight Pagans* (1990), p. 117.
5. N. K. Chadwick, *St. Columba* (Iona, 1963), pp. 4-5. See Ian Finlay, *Columba* (1992), p. 50 on the dating of *Columba: An Old Irish Life*. I am indebted to Professor Donald McIntyre for the loan of the Thomas Nelson edition of *Adomnan's Life of Columba*.
6. Ian Finlay, op. cit., pp. 53-54, 67, 103, 104, 119.
7. Ibid., pp. 122, 142; Streit, op. cit., pp. 174-76; Shirley Taulson, *Celtic Journeys* (1985), p. 111; A. Lang, *A History of Scotland* (second edition, 1900), vol. 1, p. 29; N. K. Chadwick, op. cit., pp. 12-13.
8. Finlay, op. cit., p. 182.
9. *Adomnan's Life of Columba*, editors O. A. and M. O. Anderson (Thomas Nelson, 1961), p. 523.
10. Finlay, op. cit., pp. 183-184.
11. Ibid., pp. 188, 191.

Chapter 5

CELTS IN THE WEST

When Pope Gregory I took over the See of Rome in AD 590 he wrote this to Patriarch John in Constantinople:
"Unworthy and weak as I am, I have taken over an old ship, much damaged by the waves. The waves pour in on every side, and its rotten timbers, beaten daily by continental storms, proclaim with their moans shipwreck and sinking."[1]

Was it just the independent Christianity of Ireland, Scotland and Northumbria that had so scared the emerging papacy?

No. Much more.

Celtic Christianity had swept across Europe in the fifth century and left the Roman Church, with its claims to universality, in acute crisis.

The period between the departure of the Romans and the coming of the Saxons saw Celtic Christianity come into its own in South Britain. In the century in which Columba was about his great work in the north, "Irish monks" with their veneration of the Scriptures were bringing Christ to the rest of the British Isles. They were Christendom's elite corps. They "changed Christianity into a powerful new shape".[2]

Since the terms "Irish" and "Celtic" were used interchangeably, not all the "Irish monks" had crossed the Irish Sea. The "Arthurian Age" that followed the British defeat of the Saxons on Mount Badon at the dawn of the sixth century witnessed the work of David in Wales. David and Cadoc, both members of a royal house, with Illtyd of Brittany (active from AD

475 to 535) and Mungo, fresh from soulwinning triumphs on the Clyde, built up Christian settlements in Llantwit Major, Bangor Is-y-Coed, Caldey Island, Llancarvan, Dyfed and Clwyd. The Age of the Saints – the centuries of the dominance of the Celtic Church over the religion and culture of Wales – is regarded as the most formative in the entire history of the principality.[3]

The heathen Saxons extended their conquests westwards as the sixth and seventh centuries progressed. The incursions of Danes and Vikings followed. Christian Celts migrated west before the invaders. In this way Wales and the west of England came to have the heaviest concentration of Celtic Christians.

Few places were beyond the menace of Viking raids. With Iona and Lindisfarne razed, Dunkeld on the Tay became a major Celtic centre: until the Vikings made their way up the Tay. . . .

All over Ireland, round towers like those at Glendalough became essential Celtic Christian defensive features against marauders. Some survived; at least one survives in Scotland – on the site of the ancient Celtic settlement at Abernethy.

Round tower located in Glendalough

But increasingly the topography of Wales and the extreme west of England afforded the best defence for Celtic Christianity. All of which explains why Cornwall, with its strong ties with Brittany, became, arguably, the last fastness for the Celts. It was not only proof against invaders but, apparently, insulated from the Romanising influence of Augustine's successors and the post-pagan Saxons. While a Celtic settlement in the Yeo Valley – where Sherborne Abbey now stands – fell to Cenwalch, Saxon King of Wessex, in AD 658, Cornwall's conquest did not come until the time of Athelstan in the tenth century.

Not that Celtic Christianity *came* late to Cornwall; it just left late. If, indeed, it left at all. . . . "The ruins of a Celtic monastery amid the spectacular scenery of Tintagel on the North Cornwall coast were associated by later legends with King Arthur, but are in fact the foundations of a monastery built *before 500, the oldest known monastery in the British Isles.*"[4]

The saints after whom the Cornish have named their towns as well as their churches are,

Tintagel Castle, Cornwall

almost to a person, Celtic. Most parish churches in Cornwall are built on the sites of Celtic shrines. The same remoteness that enabled Celtic Christianity to prosper in Cornwall also distanced that Celtic county from both Catholicism and Anglicanism until the nineteenth century. The Celtic evangelisation of Cornwall in the fifth century did not see its parallel until the Methodist evangelisation in the eighteenth century.

Excavations at Tintagel have turned up a chapel dedicated to St. Piran, Cornwall's patron saint. Nearby, the Institute of Cornish

Studies has recently discovered that the mounds formerly thought of as "earthworks" were, in fact, Celtic burial mounds from the fifth century. The Celtic stone coffins are now on show. Peter Berresford Ellis estimates that there were ninety-eight monastic foundations in Cornwall during the Celtic period.

Holywell seashore, Cornwall

Further excavations have been undertaken near Perranporth ("Piran's Port"). In the midst of Penhale Sands, inland from Perran Bay, archaeologists have excavated Piran's Oratory. After the excavations had been photographed, the archaeologists gave orders that this cradle of Cornwall's Christianity was to be covered over by a mound of sand. The mound is marked by a tall concrete cross. While the medieval *Life of St. Piran* is unreliable, evidence exists to connect this friend of tin miners with both South Wales and Brittany. Relics of St. Piran, including his skull, staff and bell, were preserved until well after the Reformation. Sadly it was the Reformation that destroyed the best primary historical sources about the Cornish saints; the *Lives* of the saints were destroyed with the monasteries where they had been kept.[5]

References to Cornish saints in the Celtic sources represent only fragments of information. Petroc, for example, originated at one of the North British Celtic sites, and fled to Cornwall following the destruction of the Celtic settlement in the Yeo Valley. Padstow (Petroc's stow) was the Cornish centre of his missionary activities, and churches on both sides of the Camel Estuary are dedicated to him.

Gwinear, who, having sailed from Ireland, landed in the Hayle estuary, became a martyr.[6] Mawgan is believed to have come from Wales in the early sixth century and to have been related to both David and Cadoc. He is known to have preached in Brittany as well as in Cornwall. He claimed to have been a disciple of Patrick.

Three place names in Cornwall incorporate Columba. This may be accounted for by the acknowledged dominance of Iona's Columba over the Celtic Church or by the fact that, both during and after Columba's time, his name, or derivations of it, were given to a number of great Celtic missionaries. The legend associated with St. Columba Major, which has Columba as a woman, is actually borrowed from Spain.

Austell, a contemporary of Columba, trained in Brittany and crossed Cornwall with Mewen, another Cornish saint.

Above everything else the Celtic Church was known for its extraordinary missionary zeal. By the end of the sixth century this had taken the Celts clean across Europe. It was this missionary zeal – specifically the "Irish invasion of Gaul" – that led Pope Gregory to perceive independent Celtic Christianity as a serious challenge.[7]

Irish Celtic leader Columbanus (c. AD 540-615) of Bangor, County Down, personified both the missionary vision and the "Irish Christian concept of freedom" Rome so resented. After Bangor, he had trained under Columba on Iona. His missionary journeys did not begin until he was 55, but took in Brittany, Burgundy, The Vosges, Switzerland, Lake Constance and eventually Milan. Columbanus stirred up the Gallo-Frankish branch of the Roman Church to resentment and hostilities.

> Above everything else the Celtic Church was known for its extraordinary missionary zeal. By the end of the sixth century this had taken the Celts clean across Europe.

The arrival of Augustine and eighty Benedictine monks in southern England was part of the papal contribution to the same counter-Celtic movement. By July AD 598 the Celts were in retreat; Pope Gregory was reporting in a letter that Augustine, having established a base at Canterbury, had baptised 10,000 Anglo-Saxons. Historians have asserted the improbability that so many "heathens" could have been converted so soon; they were rebaptising Celtic Christians into the Roman Church.[8]

In all the correspondence passing back and forth between Rome and Gaul, and Rome and Canterbury, one thing was emerging. The things deeply resented about Celtic Christianity were the peculiarly "Irish customs". Included in these "customs" were liturgies, religious observances and rites of baptism. Columbanus and his followers were said "to accept nothing outside the apostolical doctrine", "denying the Pope's jurisdiction". Augustine and his successors were out to destroy the Celtic Church and its "distinctives".[9]

And destroy them they did. Southern Ireland threw in its lot with the Italian mission in AD 632, Northern Ireland in 695, Northumbria at the Council of Whitby in 664.

The Celtic Church in Scotland felt the heavy hand of King Nectan. In AD 717 he banished the Columbate brethren from their island retreat on Iona.

The Celtic Church in the West of England surrendered in AD 768, though this surrender does not appear to have affected Cornwall.

In the mountains of Wales, Celtic Christianity held out the longest. Wales accepted Catholicism in AD 777.[10]

The Celtic Church "distinctives" did not die when the kings and chieftains accepted Roman authority. Accusations of "heresy" and "separatism" continued to be fired from the Vatican at the Celtic lands for centuries to come. "Wales in particular clung tenaciously to her old traditions long after the other Celtic countries had joined the Roman Order." And, in the nomenclature of the Celtic centuries, curiously, "Wales" included Cornwall and other parts of the West of England.[11]

So, what were the distinctives of the Church of Patrick and Columba that made it so imperative that they be destroyed?

REFERENCES:

1. Jakob Streit, *Sun and Cross: From Megalithic Culture to Early Christianity in Ireland* (1993), p. 195.

2. D. L. Edwards, *Christian England* (revised edition, 1989), pp. 27-28.

3. N. K. Chadwick, *Studies in the Early British Church* (1954), pp. 4-13; E. G. Bowen, *The Settlements of the Celtic Saints in Wales* (University of Wales, 1954), pp. ix, 1-5, 6, 7, 19, 25, 35, 41, 43-48, 117.

4. Edwards, op. cit., pp. 28, 40; G. H. Doble, *The Cornish Saints Series*, nos. 1-48, Institute of Historical Research; S. Baring Gould, *Lives of the British Saints* (1907), vols. I, II and III; Peter Berresford Ellis, op. cit., pp. 61-68.

5. Peter Berresford Ellis, *Celtic Inheritance* (Constable, 1992), p. 61.

6. Ibid., p. 62.

7. Streit, op. cit., pp. 195, 196.

8. Streit, op. cit., pp. 179-191, 196-197.

9. Ibid.; J. Healy, *The Ancient Irish Church* (1892), p. 59; A. Lang, *A History of Scotland* (second edition, 1900), vol. I, pp. 34-35.

10. Leslie Hardinge, *The Celtic Church in Britain* (1972), pp. xii-xiii; A. Lang, op. cit., pp. 35-36; N. K. Chadwick, *The Age of the Saints* (SPCK, 1961), pp. 5-7.

11. N. K. Chadwick, op. cit., pp. 65-66, 70; Hugh Williams, *Christianity in Early Britain* (1912), p. 441 et seq.

Chapter 6

THE CELTIC DISTINCTIVES

One of the Celtic distinctives was causing concern to a Scottish queen as late as the eleventh century.

Queen Margaret, later *Saint* Margaret, had fled to Scotland with her father, Edward Atheling, a pretender to the English throne, in 1069. Though pious by the standards of the time, she failed to repulse the advances of the (already married) King Malcolm III of Scotland. Malcolm's queen was banished, and Margaret became Queen in Malcolm's capital, Dunfermline.

Margaret was to be responsible for a massive shift away from Celtic religious observances in Scotland. Ian Finlay comments:

"While the greatness of Queen Margaret is not to be denied, it is remarkable how fervid Scots today will take her side with eloquence, when the contemporary evidence shows that the Scots of the year 1093 hated everything she stood for, and that Donald Bane had the entire Celtic kingdom behind him when he came claiming the crown. . . . That Margaret had brought many of the blessings of southern civilisation with her from the Saxon court to Scotland is undeniable, but it is only one side of the case – a people, like a man, may be excused if it resents blessings when it has to pay for them with cherished possessions."[1]

What were these "cherished possessions"?

Soon the new queen was writing to her English cousins expressing astonishment at the religious practices of the Scots. Among the "peculiarities" of the Scots was that "they work on Sunday, but keep Saturday in a sabbatical manner". To another correspondent she complained, "They are accustomed also to neglect reverence for the Lord's days (Sundays); and thus to continue upon them as upon other days all the labours of earthly work."[2]

The observance of the Saturday Sabbath by most Scots went hand in hand with their refusal to "recognise the overlordship of the Pope in matters spiritual". Despite the best efforts of King Nectan centuries earlier, Scottish Christianity was still of the "Columban" or "Celtic", not the "Roman", variety.

The most popular narrative history of Scotland – *Scotland: A Concise History* by P. Hume Brown (Langsyne) – confirms that, at Margaret's accession, "the people worked on Sundays and observed Saturday as the Sabbath day." Peter Berresford Ellis in *Celtic Inheritance* writes: "When Rome began to take a particular interest in the Celtic Church towards the end of the sixth century AD there were several differences between them. . . . The Celtic Sabbath was celebrated on a Saturday." Ellis's comment covers the Celtic Church in Wales, Ireland, Cornwall and Gaul, as well as Scotland. Romanism was, apparently, coming into Scotland but had no strength north of the Forth.[3]

> Among the "peculiarities" of the Scots was that "they work on Sunday, but keep Saturday in a sabbatical manner".

This gave Queen Margaret her crusade (and her route to canonisation): "Margaret did all she could to make the Scottish clergy do and believe exactly what the Church of Rome commanded."[4] This involved the enforcement of Sunday-keeping, a policy continued by her son, King David I. Nevertheless, on the eve of the Reformation, there were still many communities in the Scottish Highlands loyal to the seventh-day Sabbath, as opposed to "the Papal Sunday".[5]

Two books published in 1963 – to commemorate Columba's landing at Iona in AD 563 – concerned themselves with the "Celtic distinctives" and counted among them the observance of the seventh-day Sabbath. Dr. W. D. Simpson published *The Historical St. Columba* in Edinburgh. He confirms that Columba and his companions kept "the day of the Sabbath" and, in case there should be any doubt, adds in a footnote "Saturday, of course."[6]

Rev. F. W. Fawcett was commissioned to write his *Columba – Pilgrim for Christ* by the Lord Bishop of Derry and Raphoe. His book was published in Londonderry and printed by the *Derry Standard* in connection with the Irish commemoration of Columba's mission. Fawcett outlines eight Celtic distinctives: among these that the Celts had a married priesthood and that they observed the seventh day as the Sabbath.[7]

The reason why Pope Gregory I had perceived the Celtic Church as such a major threat and why he and his successors expended such efforts in destroying the distinctive "Irish customs" became massively evident.

A. O. Anderson and M. O. Anderson, in the introduction to their *Adomnan's Life of Columba*, shed light not only on Columba's seventh-day Sabbath-keeping practice, but on the gradual "adjustment" of manuscripts by generations of Roman copyists in an attempt to provide an impression that the Celtic saints held Sunday sacred.

Adomnan's use of *sabbatum* for Saturday, the seventh day of the week, is a clear indication from "Columba's mouth" that "Sabbath was not Sunday. Sunday, the first day of the week, is 'Lord's-day'. Adomnan's attitude to Sunday is important, because he wrote at a time when there was controversy over the question of whether the ritual of the biblical Sabbath was to be transferred to the Christians' Lord's-day."[8]

> The observance of the Saturday Sabbath by most Scots went hand in hand with their refusal to "recognise the overlordship of the Pope in matters spiritual".

The Old Testament required seventh-day Sabbath observance, and, reason *Adomnan*'s editors, since the New Testament nowhere repealed the fourth commandment, the seventh day was observed by all early Christians. The evidence they adduce suggests that no actual confusion between Sunday and "the Sabbath" occurred until the early sixth century, and then in the writings of the rather obscure Caesarius of Arles.[9]

"In England, the question of Sunday may have been among the 'other ecclesiastical matters' discussed by the Synod of Whitby in 664," reason the Andersons, in addition to the date of Easter, which could not have caused such a rift. A *weekly*, not just *yearly*, observance separated the Celts from the Romans. But the Romans had the task of writing the history of the Church and of copying the writings of Church fathers. While those who copied the Scriptures appear to have been constrained by the Scriptural injunction not to add or take away from the words of the Book, and, in the main, to have done a conscientious job, the same scruples did not apply when they copied out the writings of the Church fathers. As the centuries progressed, the writings of the Celtic saints, including Patrick, were "amended" to convey the impression that the saints held Sunday sacred, whereas, in the earliest version of their manuscripts, it is clear that they observed the seventh-day Sabbath.[10]

The Roman "movement" to supersede the Celtic Sabbath with Sunday "culminated in the production of an (apocryphal) 'Letter of Jesus', or 'Letter of Lord's-day', alleged to have been found on the altar of Peter in Rome; and it is said in the annals to have been brought to Ireland by a pilgrim (c. 886). Upon this basis, laws were promulgated, imposing heavy penalties for those that violated on Sunday certain regulations derived from Jewish prohibitions for Sabbath. . . . There is in fact no historical evidence that Ninian, or Patrick, or Columba, or any of their contemporaries in Ireland, kept Sunday as a Sabbath."[11]

> The seventh-day Sabbath, enjoined by the fourth of the Ten Commandments, had been observed by Jesus, and nowhere in Scripture had its sacredness been diminished or transferred to another day.

The seventh-day Sabbath, enjoined by the fourth of the Ten Commandments, had been observed by Jesus, and nowhere in Scripture had its sacredness been diminished or transferred to another day.[12] Over centuries several factors had combined to induce Christians in some parts of the Roman Empire to neglect the observance of the Sabbath in favour of Sunday.[13]

After the fall of Jerusalem, AD 70, and the crushing of the Bar Kokhba revolt in AD 135, the mood in many parts of the Empire was frostily antisemitic. To distance themselves from the Sabbath-keeping Jews, some communities of Christians moved over to Sunday observance. Only in later centuries, however, was the "day of resurrection" rationalisation thought of. At the time the choice of Sunday was influenced more by sun worship of Mithraism, widely prevalent in the Empire.[14]

When, on 7 March 321, the Emperor Constantine decreed the observance of the "venerable day of the Sun" in place of the Sabbath, he was confirming a practice already followed by the majority of Christians.

Nevertheless, in some parts of the Empire, from which Rome was remote, and in which antisemitism was less evident, records indicate that the Saturday Sabbath was still observed. In still other areas both Saturday and Sunday were observed as "sabbaths". It was to counter this practice that the Council of Laodicea in AD 364 ruled that the seventh-day Sabbath should be deliberately desecrated.[15]

After both Dr. W. D. Simpson and Rev. F. W. Fawcett had, in 1963, gone into print with the view that the evidence of primary sources indicated that Columba and his companions kept "the day of the Sabbath", Leslie Hardinge decided to examine every primary source connected with the Celtic saints to find out if the Sabbath-Celtic connection was valid. His research occupied him for many years. Eventually he brought his findings together in a dissertation for which the University of London awarded him a PhD degree. In 1972, in more readable form, the Society for Promoting Christian Knowledge (SPCK) published Dr. Hardinge's findings in *The Celtic Church in Britain*.

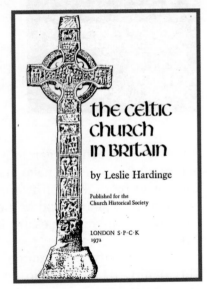

the celtic church in Britain

by Leslie Hardinge

Published for the
Church Historical Society

LONDON S·P·C·K
1972

The upshot of Hardinge's research?

The Sabbath-Celtic connection was a firm one.

There is significant evidence that Patrick observed the seventh-day Sabbath before his theological training at Auxerre.[16] Hence it may be conjectured that the practice had been present since childhood – he was a third-generation Christian clergyman – or that Patrick had acquired the Sabbath-keeping habit from the Copts at Lerins.

Patrick's practice of seventh-day Sabbath observance was an important part of his missionary creed in Ireland (where no antisemitic prejudice was present to stigmatise it). Elsewhere Christendom was mixed in its observances; but the decrees of Constantine carried no weight in Ireland.

The *Senchus Mor*, the ancient Irish legal system framed with the help of Patrick, would appear actually to have enshrined seventh-day Sabbath observance as well as defining capital offences, the rules governing the relationship between master and servant, etc.[17] For any manuscript linking Patrick with Sunday-sacredness we have to look to a period over 500 years after the saint's death.

In the earliest manuscripts of the "Rule of Columcille" (Columba) (see *Appendix B*) item five reads: "The seventh day was observed as the Sabbath." Eighty years after Columba's death the sabbatical Sunday had not been accepted on Iona. Though we cannot assume uniformity of practice over the many Columban settlements, Archbishop Theodore, one of Augustine's successors (like Queen Margaret, centuries later), inveighed against the Celts for their seventh-day Sabbath observance.[18]

> It was one thing for kings to make an accommodation with Rome, but quite another to root Celtic Christian customs out of the lives of people.

As with Patrick, there is evidence that David observed the seventh-day Sabbath from sunset Friday evening. The Welsh patron saint also preached and celebrated communion on Sunday.[19]

As the various segments of the Celtic Church accepted assimilation into the Roman communion, so the shift from Sabbath to Sunday observance – which had taken place centuries earlier in other parts of Europe – began to take place in Ireland and the Celtic portions of Britain. However, as Queen Margaret discovered in the eleventh century, it was one thing for kings to make an accommodation with Rome, but quite another to root Celtic Christian customs out of the lives of people. In the glens of Scotland, and in the distant coves of Cornwall, the biblical Sabbath brought more blessing than Constantine's "venerable day of the Sun".

In his twenty-year examination of the primary sources of Celtic Christianity, Dr. Leslie Hardinge turned up other Celtic distinctives. Fundamental to all, he found, was a deep love and veneration for the Scriptures. He found ringing passages in the writings of Patrick and Columba in which they envisioned the literal Second Advent of Jesus. He discovered that the Celtic attitude was such that all life was governed by the Ten Commandments; it was not just the fourth that was held in reverence. He was especially thrilled as he pieced together the doctrine of salvation held by the Celtic Church.

For the great Celtic teachers man was not saved "by the merits of his deeds, but by God and His grace". Salvation was by grace though faith in the merits of the Christ of Calvary. Law-keeping was the fruit, not the route of salvation to the Celtic Christians; the effect, not the cause of salvation. The Cause of salvation was Christ alone.[20]

Another "Celtic distinctive" stressed by modern authorities – and derived originally from Lerins – was baptism by immersion.[21]

Pope Gregory I and his successors perceived the Celtic Church as a threat and set about its destruction. If, instead, they had sought to learn from it, there need never have been a Reformation.

And who can tell what blessings would have come to the lives of Christian believers if they had embraced the Sabbath of the Celts, the Sabbath of which Jesus is Lord?

Old Library of Trinity College, Dublin

REFERENCES:

1. Ian Finlay, *Scotland* (Oxford University Press, 1945), p. 28.

2. A. Lang, *History of Scotland* (second edition, 1900), vol. 1, p. 96; Turgot's *Life of Queen Margaret* (circa 1100), p. xix – cited W. Forbes-Leith, Turgot's *Life of Queen Margaret* (Edinburgh, 1896). See Professor W. F. Skene, *Celtic Scotland* (Edinburgh, 1886-90), vol. 2, pp. 248-249.

3. (Revised edition, 1990), p. 33; Peter Berresford Ellis, *Celtic Inheritance* (Constable, 1985), p. 45.

4. P. Hume Brown, *Scotland: A Concise History*, pp. 48-49.

5. A. Lang, op. cit.; W. F. Skene, op. cit.

6. W. D. Simpson, *The Historical St. Columba* (1963), pp. 70, 120 (item 75).

7. F. W. Fawcett, *Columba – Pilgrim for Christ* (Londonderry, 1963), p. 9.

8. A. O. and M. O. Anderson (eds.) *Adomnan's Life of Columba* (Thomas Nelson's Medieval Texts, 1961), pp. 25-26.

9. Ibid., p. 26.

10. Ibid., pp. 26-28.

11. Ibid., p. 28.

12. Exodus 20; Luke 4:16-19; Leslie Hardinge, *The Celtic Church in Britain* (1972), p. 75; Samuele Bacchiocchi, *From Sabbath to Sunday: A Historical Investigation of the Rise of Sunday Observance in Early Christianity* (Pontifical Gregorian University Press, Rome, 1977).

13. Bacchiocchi, op. cit.

14. G. L. Laing, *Survivals of Roman Religion* (London, 1931), p. 148.

15. Hardinge, op. cit., p. 76.

16. Ibid., pp. 77-79.

17. Ibid., p. 80. The four manuscripts of the text of the *Liber ex Lege Moisi* are extant. Their import is summarised in the appendix to Hardinge (pp. 207-216).

18. Ibid., pp. 82-83, 84.

19. Ibid., pp. 81-82.

20. Ibid., pp. 65-66.

21. N. K. Chadwick, *The Age of the Saints in the Celtic Church* (Oxford University Press, 1961), pp. 67-68.

Appendix A

HISTORICAL BACKGROUND TO THE SABBATH CONTROVERSY

The seventh-day Sabbath was carefully observed by the Hebrews throughout the Old Testament period. Jesus and His disciples kept the Sabbath in obedience to a gracious heavenly Father. Throughout the first century, both Jewish and Gentile converts to Christianity observed the Sabbath.

Several factors combined to induce Christians to give up the Sabbath in favour of Sunday in the succeeding centuries. After the fall of Jerusalem in AD 70 and the crushing of the Jewish revolt against the Romans in AD 135, the Jews scattered throughout the Roman Empire. Their name and religion were strongly opposed. In most circles a Jew was considered *persona non grata*.

One of the most obvious outward marks of a Jew was the keeping of the Sabbath. Pagan religions throughout the centuries had placed special significance on sun worship. Sun worship was common in Egypt, Babylon, Persia and Rome. It is not surprising that early Christian leaders, attempting to disassociate themselves from Judaism as well as to make Christianity more acceptable to Rome, saw the observance of the 'day of the sun' – the first day of the week – as a bridge.

Sun worship gradually grew in prominence throughout the Roman Empire. Although initially opposed, the third-century Roman Emperor Aurelian, who reigned from AD 270 to 275, strongly supported sun worship. By the early fourth century the Emperor Constantine, who made Christianity the "official" religion of the Empire, passed a Sunday observance law on 7 March 321, calling Sunday "the venerable day of the sun". Church and state leaders gradually united to shift the emphasis from the biblical Sabbath to its substitute day.

However, Sabbath observance was still practised. Some Christian champions were unwilling to surrender the claims of God upon their conscience. To them, the Sabbath was more than a matter of days. It was an issue of obedience to God.

SABBATH OBSERVANCE

Historical references through the centuries

Used with permission from Mark A. Finley's *The Almost Forgotten Day* (1988), pp. 55-84.

Through the centuries after Constantine there was always a section of Christianity – usually a small minority – who stayed faithful to the seventh-day Sabbath.

FIRST TO FIFTH CENTURIES AD

A careful study of the historical sources extant from the first to fifth centuries reveals the fact that the transference of the sacredness of the biblical Sabbath to Sunday was a long and gradual process. Dr. Kenneth Strand, Professor of Church History at Andrews University, Berrien Springs, Michigan, categorically states, "Until the second century there is no concrete evidence of a Christian weekly Sunday celebration anywhere. The first specific references during that century come from Alexandria and Rome, places that also rejected the observance of the seventh-day Sabbath." *The Sabbath in Scripture and History* (Review and Herald, 1982), p. 330.

Why did both Alexandria and Rome surrender the seventh-day Sabbath earlier than most cities?

The answer can be found in an understanding of early Christianity. New Testament Christianity was largely composed of converted Jews. Later, thousands of Gentiles flocked into the Church. While the early Christians faithfully upheld the claims of the Ten Commandments by observing the seventh-day Sabbath, these new converts, whose background was tainted with sun worship, were more likely to surrender the Sabbath. The centres of Christianity shifted from Jerusalem to Alexandria and Rome. Gentile converts who did not have the same regard for the Sabbath, and who were strongly influenced by a background of sun worship (and, later, the rationalisation that Jesus had risen from the dead on a Sunday), accepted the compromise measures more easily.

The situation in Alexandria and Rome was not typical of all cities in the Empire. Fifth-century church historian Socrates Scholasticus provides this insight: "For almost all churches throughout the world celebrate the sacred mysteries (the Lord's Supper) *on the Sabbath* of every week. Yet Christians at Alexandria and Rome, on account of some ancient tradition, have ceased to do this. The Egyptians in the neighbourhood of Alexandria and the inhabitants of Thebais *hold their religious assemblies on the Sabbath.*" (Italics supplied.) Socrates Scholasticus, *Ecclesiastical History*, 5.22 (NPNF/22:132). "The people of Constantinople and *almost everywhere assembled together on the Sabbath*, as well as on the first day of the week, which custom is never observed at Rome or Alexandria." (Italics supplied.) Reference Sozomen, *Ecclesiastical History*, 7.19 (NPNF 2/2:390).

The shift from Sabbath to Sunday was gradual. When Sunday first emerged in Christian circles it continued to be a day of work, but included some form of worship service. It did not immediately replace the Sabbath, as the above quotations reveal. For 200 years (AD 100-300) Sunday observance existed side by side with Sabbath observance. But the trend set by Constantine and others eventually led to the change of the Sabbath to Sunday.

In many places there was stiff resistance to this change. Existing historical documents reveal a deep interest in seventh-day Sabbath worship.

FIRST CENTURY AD

Josephus. "There is not any city of the Grecians, nor any of the barbarians, nor any nation whatsoever, whither our custom of resting on the seventh day hath not come!" Cited M'Clatchie, *Notes and Queries on China and Japan*, edited by Dennys, vol. 4, nos. 7 and 8, p. 100.

First-century Christians. "The spiritual seed of Abraham fled to Pella, on the other side of Jordan, where they found a safe place of refuge, and could serve their Master and keep His Sabbath." Eusebius, *Ecclesiastical History*, book 3, chapter 5.

Philo. Declares the seventh day to be a festival, not of this or that city, but of the universe. Cited M'Clatchie, *Notes and Queries*, vol. 4, p. 99.

SECOND CENTURY AD

Early Christians. "The primitive Christians had a great veneration for the Sabbath, and spent the day in devotion and sermons. And it is not to be doubted that they derived this practice from the apostles themselves, as appears by several scriptures to that purpose." Dr. T. H. Morer, a Church of England divine writing in 1701, *Dialogues on the Lord's Day* (London, 1701), p. 189.

"... The Sabbath was a strong tie which united them with the life of the whole people, and in keeping the Sabbath holy they followed not only the example but also the command of Jesus." *Geschichte des Sonntags*, pp. 13, 14.

Many Gentile Christians also observed the Sabbath. Gieseler,

Church History, vol. 1, ch. 2, p. 93, par. 30.

"The primitive Christians did keep the Sabbath of the Jews; . . . therefore the Christians, for a long time together, did keep their conventions upon the Sabbath, in which some portions of the Law were read: and this continued till the time of the Laodicean Council." *The Whole Works of Jeremy Taylor*, vol. IX, p. 416, R. Heber's edition, vol. XII, p. 416.

"It is certain that the ancient Sabbath did remain and was observed together with the celebration of the Lord's day by the Christians of the East Church, about 300 years after our Saviour's death." *A Learned Treatise of the Sabbath*, p. 77. Note: by "Lord's day" the writer here is referring to Sunday as distinct from the seventh-day Sabbath.

THIRD CENTURY AD

Egypt. Oxrhynchus Papyrus, AD 200-250. "Except ye make the Sabbath a real sabbath (Greek: *sabbatize the Sabbath*), ye shall not see the Father." *The Oxrhynchus Papyrie*, part 1, p. 3, Logion 2, verso 4-11, London: Offices of the Egyptian Exploration Fund, 1898.

Early Christians. "The seventh-day Sabbath was . . . solemnised by Christ, the apostles, and primitive Christians, till the Laodicean Council did in a manner quite abolish the observances of it." *Dissertation on the Lord's Day*, pp. 33, 34, 44.

Palestine to China (Church of the East). As early as AD 225 there existed large bishoprics of the Church of the East (Sabbath-keeping) stretching from Palestine to India. Mingana, *Early Spread of Christianity*, vol. 10, p. 460.

FOURTH CENTURY AD

Italy and the East. "It was the practice generally of the Eastern churches; and some churches of the West. . . . For in the Church of Milan; . . . it seems that Saturday was held in far esteem. . . . Not that the Eastern churches, or any of the rest which observed that day, were inclined to Judaism; but they came together on the Sabbath day, to worship Jesus Christ the Lord of the Sabbath." *History of the Sabbath*, part 2, pp. 73, 74, par. 5. Dr. Heylyn, London, 1636.

Council of Laodicea. AD 365.

"Canon 16 – On Saturday the Gospels and other portions of the Scripture shall be read aloud."

"Canon 29 – Christians shall not Judaise and be idle on Saturday, but shall work on that day; but the Lord's day they shall especially honour, and, as being Christians, shall, if possible, do no work on that day." Hefele's *Councils*, vol. 2, p. 6.

The Council of Laodicea was an Eastern gathering which represented Greek Orthodox attitude. An Eastern Church was revising the celebration of the Lord's Supper on the Sabbath at about the time this council was held. The Council of Laodicea attests to the re-establishment of Sabbath observance in the East. This was one factor which led to the split in Eastern and Western branches of Christianity.

Abyssinia. "In the last half of that century St. Ambrose of Milan stated officially that the Abyssinian Bishop, Museus, had 'travelled almost everywhere in the country of the Seres (China)'. For more than seventeen centuries the Abyssinian church continued to sanctify Saturday as the holy day of the fourth commandment." Ambrose, de Moribus, *Brachmanorium Opera Omnia*, 1132, found in Migne, *Patrologia Lattina*, vol. 17, pp. 1131-1132.

The Orient. "The ancient Christians were very careful in the observation of Saturday, or the seventh day. . . . It is plain that all the Oriental churches, and the greatest part of the world, observed the Sabbath as a festival. . . . Athanasius likewise tells us that they held religious assemblies on the Sabbath, not because they were infected with Judaism, but to worship Jesus, the Lord of the Sabbath. Epiphanius says the same." *Antiquities of the Christian Church*, vol. II, Book XX, ch. 3, section 1, 66.1137, 1138.

FIFTH CENTURY AD

In Jerome's time (c. AD 420) the "devoutest" Christians did ordinary work on Sunday and continued "the observance of the Jewish Sabbath". Lyman Coleman, *Ancient Christianity Exemplified*, ch. 26, p. 527, section 2; White, Lord Bishop of Ely, *Treatise of the Sabbath Day*, p. 219.

France. "Wherefore, except vespers and nocturns, there are no public services among them in the day except on Saturday (Sabbath) and Sunday." John Cassian, a French monk, *Institutes*, book 3, ch. 2.

John Cassian promoted the observance of both Saturday and Sunday in his own monastery in the South of France. He taught that the seventh day of the week was the Sabbath of creation, written with God's own finger on tables of stone and given to the human race for all time. He refused to accept the Roman plan of observing only Sunday. Although Cassian attempted to establish the observance of the Sabbath, as well as Sunday, in France, the Roman Church authorities refused.

Nevertheless, he had significant short-term influence.

Sidonius. (Speaking of King Theodoric of the Goths, AD 454-526:) "It is a fact that it was formerly the custom of the East to keep the Sabbath in the same manner of the Lord's Day and to hold sacred assemblies: while, on the other hand, the people of the West, contending for the Lord's day, have neglected the celebration of the Sabbath." *Apollinaris Sidonii Epistolse*, lib. 1, 2; Migne, 57.

Constantinople. "The people of Constantinople, and almost everywhere, assembled together on the Sabbath, as well as on the first day of the week, which custom is never observed at Rome or at Alexandria." Socrates, op. cit., book 7, ch. 19.

Egypt. "There are several cities and villages in Egypt where, contrary to the usage established elsewhere, the people meet together on Sabbath evenings, and, although they have dined previously, partake of the Lord's Supper." Sozomen, *Ecclesiastical History*, book 7, ch. 19.

Pope Innocent (AD 402-417). Pope Sylvester (314-335) was the first pontiff to order the churches to fast on Saturday, and Pope Innocent made it a binding law in the churches that obeyed him. This was done in a deliberate attempt to bring the Sabbath into disfavour.

"Innocentius did ordain the Saturday or Sabbath to be always fasted." Cited Peter Heylyn, *History of the Sabbath*, part 2, ch. 2, p. 44.

SIXTH CENTURY AD

Scottish Church. "In this latter instance they seemed to have followed a custom of which we find traces in the early monastic Church of Ireland by which they held Saturday to be the Sabbath on which they rested from all their labours." W. F. Skene, *Adomnan's Life of St. Columba* (1874), p. 96.

Scotland and Ireland. "We seem to see here an allusion to the custom, observed in the early monastic Church of Ireland, of keeping the day of rest on Saturday, or the Sabbath." Bellesheim, *History of the Catholic Church in Scotland*, vol. 1, p. 86.

SEVENTH CENTURY AD

Scotland and Ireland. James C. Moffatt, Professor of Church History at Princeton: "It seems to have been customary in the Celtic churches of early times, in Ireland as well as Scotland, to keep Saturday, the Jewish Sabbath, as a day of rest from labour. They observed the fourth commandment literally upon the seventh day of the week." *The Church in Scotland*, p. 140.

"The Celts used the Latin Bible unlike the Vulgate and kept Saturday as the day of rest, with special religious services on Sunday." Flick, *The Rise of the Medieval Church*, p. 237.

Rome. Pope Gregory I (AD 590-604) wrote against "Roman citizens (who) forbid any work being done on the Sabbath day". *Nicene and Post-Nicene Fathers*, second series, vol. XIII, p. 13, epist. 1.

"Gregory, Bishop by the grace of God to his well-beloved sons, the Roman citizens: It has come to me that certain men of perverse spirit have disseminated among you things depraved and opposed to the holy faith, so that they forbid anything to be done on the day of the Sabbath. What shall I call them except preachers of antichrist?" *Epistles*, B.13:1.

EIGHTH CENTURY AD

Council of Liftinae, Belgium (AD 745). "The third allocution of this council warns against the observance of the Sabbath, referring to the decree of the Council of Laodicea." Hefele, *Conciliengesch*, 3. 512, section 362.

NINTH CENTURY AD

Bulgaria. "Bulgaria in the early season of its evangelisation had been taught that no work should be performed on the Sabbath." A response to Pope Nicholas I, *Responsum 10*, found in Mansi, *Sacrorum Concilorum Nova et Amplissima Collectio*, vol. 15, p. 406.

TENTH AND ELEVENTH CENTURIES AD

Scotland. "It was another custom of theirs to neglect the reverence due to the Lord's day, by devoting themselves to every kind of worldly business upon it, just as they did upon other days. That this was contrary to the law, she (Queen Margaret) proved to them as well by reason as by authority. 'Let us venerate the Lord's day,' said she, 'because of the resurrection of our Lord, which happened upon that day, and let us no longer do servile works upon it; bearing in mind that upon this day we were redeemed from the slavery of the devil. The blessed Pope Gregory affirms the same.' " Turgot, *Life of Margaret*, p. 49 (British Museum Library).

"Queen Margaret's next point was that they did not duly reverence the Lord's day, but in this latter instance they seemed to have followed a custom of which we find traces in the early churches of Ireland, by which they held Saturday to be the Sabbath on which they rested from all their labours." W. F. Skene, *Celtic Scotland*, vol. 2, p. 349.

T. Ratcliffe Barnett, in his book on the fervent Catholic queen of Scotland who, in 1060, was first to attempt the ruin of Columba's brethren, writes: "In this matter the Scots had perhaps kept up the traditional usage of the ancient Irish Church which observed

Saturday instead of Sunday as the day of rest." T. Ratcliffe Barnet, *Margaret of Scotland: Queen and Saint*, p. 97.

Greek Church. "The observance of Saturday is, as everyone knows, the subject of a bitter dispute between the Greeks and the Latins." Neale, *A History of the Early Eastern Church*, vol. 1, p. 731. Note: This refers to the separation of the Greek and Roman Churches in 1054.

Alpine region. Even during the height of persecution by the papal power during the Middle Ages the Sabbath was not totally forgotten as a day of rest. There is no firm historical evidence that all the Waldenses kept the Saturday Sabbath. Nevertheless, it is clear that some did. From their mountain hide-outs in southern France and northern Italy, they descended on the cities of France, Switzerland and Italy disguised as merchants. Constantly alert for potential converts, they often shared, at the risk of their lives, handwritten Bible manuscripts which they had carefully sewn into their long, flowing robes. Dr. Daniel Augsberger of Andrews University makes this interesting observation regarding the Waldenses: "It is interesting to note that instances of Sabbath-keeping occur where the Waldenses had preached with the greatest success." Daniel Augsberger, *The Sabbath in Scripture and History* (Review and Herald, 1982), p. 208.

TWELFTH CENTURY AD

Lombardy. "Traces of Sabbath-keepers are found in the times of Gregory I, Gregory VII and in the twelfth century in Lombardy." *Strong's Encyclopedia*, vol. 1, p. 660.

Waldenses. "Among the documents, we have by the same peoples an explanation of the Ten Commandments dated by Boyer 1120. Observance of the Sabbath by ceasing from worldly labours is enjoined." Blair, *History of the Waldenses*, vol. 1, p. 220.

Wales. "There is much evidence that the Sabbath prevailed in Wales universally until AD 1115, when the first Roman bishop was seated at St. David's. The old Welsh Sabbath-keeping churches did not even then altogether bow the knee to Rome, but fled to their hiding places." Lewis, *Seventh-day Baptists in Europe and America*, vol. 1, p. 29.

THIRTEENTH CENTURY AD

Waldenses. "The inquisitors . . . declare that the sign of a Vaudois, deemed worthy of death, was that he followed Christ and sought to obey the commandments of God." H. C. Lea, *History of the Inquisition of the Middle Ages*, vol. 1.

Appendix B

THE RULE OF COLUMBA

The twelve Irish monks who had come over with Columba were soon joined by Britons drawn to Iona by the fame of the abbot. Columba referred to them as The Family. The Columban rule enforced strict observance of religious duty, ascetic practice and self-denial. As in similar Irish houses, poverty, celibacy and obedience were strictly enforced, together with caution and reason in speech, humility, hospitality and kindness to animals.

Other features of the Celtic Church were:

1. The Holy Communion was given in both kinds.
2. Celtic priests seem to have been first to face the altar. Elsewhere in Christendom the western position was used.
3. A married priesthood (secular).
4. Bishops officiated in vestments of truly oriental splendour; gold and silver crowns were worn.

- Wednesdays and Fridays were fast days, and Lent was strictly observed.
- The principal service was the 'Sacred Mysteries of the Eucharist': the Holy Communion, which was celebrated on Sundays and holy days.
- The usual hours for daily prayers – Matins, Vespers, etc. – were observed.
- Compline was unknown at this time in the Celtic Church.

5. The seventh day was observed as the Sabbath.
6. The Crucifixion scene was generally absent in Celtic carvings – the Cross was depicted in native form.
7. The monks slept in separate cells instead of in one common dormitory.
8. The east window was a characteristic in early Irish churches.

This early version of *The Rule of Columba* is reproduced in *Columba – Pilgrim for Christ* by Rev. F. W. Fawcett, MA. Rev. Fawcett is a Church of Ireland clergyman. He was commissioned by the Lord Bishop of Derry and Raphoe to produce this book as part of the celebrations in 1963 of the departure of Columba for Iona in AD 563. Printed by *The Derry Standard Ltd.*, Londonderry, 1963.

The author is aware that later copyists of *The Rule of Columba* re-arranged the distinctives and either omitted item 5 or replaced it with another enjoining the observance of the first day as the "Lord's Day".

Appendix C

QUEEN MARGARET OF SCOTLAND

Alan J. Wilson's *St. Margaret Queen of Scotland* (published in Edinburgh by John Donald in 1993) accepts that "for Columba, Saturday was the Sabbath" (p. 74) and that among Margaret's "religious reforms" in eleventh-century Scotland was the enforcement of Sunday as "the Lord's Day" (pp. 75, 88).

On the Celtic Church, north of the Forth, Wilson says: "Their methods had developed from the teachings of Columba, who travelled around Scotland five centuries before St. Margaret arrived in Scotland" (p. 71). However, among the Celtic communities he believes there was a "lack of uniformity" (p. 72).